THE CONCEPT OF LIBERATION WHILE STILL ALIVE IN THE PHILOSOPHY OF MADHVA

THE CONCEPT OF LIBERATION WHILE STILL ALIVE IN THE PHILOSOPHY OF MADHVA

ROQUE MESQUITA
University of Vienna

ADITYA PRAKASHAN
New Delhi

First English version: 2007

ISBN: 978-81-7742-073-9

Published by Aditya Prakashan, Delhi – 110 009
and printed at Rajkamal Electric Press, Delhi – 110 033.

PREFACE

This paper is based on materials I collected in the beginning of the nineties in connection with my research into the concept of *jīvanmukti.* Since then two papers have been published: one on the concept of liberation in the philosophy of Kumārila (Mesquita 1994) and the other on the concept of *apavarga* according to Śrīdhara (Mesquita 1995). For the latter paper, I am indebted in a special way to Prof. Dr. Wilhelm Halbfass, visiting Professor at our Department of Indology in summer 1994, who went through my paper and made many valuable suggestions. I had the honour to make his acquaintance not only as a brilliant scholar, but also as a true friend. It is therefore, a great satisfaction for me to contribute to the Commemoration volume of Wilhelm Halbfass with a paper dedicated to the same topic as put forward by Madhva. The paper referred to here was originaly published in German under the title: *Die Idee der Erlösung bei Lebzeiten im System Madhvas* in: Karin Preisendanz (ed.), Expanding and Merging Horizons: Contributions to South Asian and Cross-Cultural Studies in Commemoration of *Wilhelm Halbfass* (Vienna: Austrian Academy of Sciences 2007: pp. 433-454). I am grateful to the original publisher Austrian Academy of Sciences for permission to print this paper in English version in India. The present translation contains slight changes and minor additions.

My sincere thanks to Prof. Dr. George Chemparathy, Emeritus Professor of Indian Philosophy at the University of Utrecht, for his useful remarks and improvements to the English expression of this paper. My special thanks are due also to Christian Ferstl, Student of Indian Philosophy at the Department of South Asian Studies at the University of Vienna, for his technical help in the electronic data processing and for preparing the camera-ready copy of the present booklet.

THE CONCEPT OF LIBERATION WHILE STILL ALIVE IN THE PHILOSOPHY OF MADHVA

The concept of liberation while alive is shared by many brahmaṇical schools, possibly under the influence of Buddhist distinction between awakening (*nirvāṇa*) of the Buddha and his final state of liberation (*parinirvāṇa*).[1] Not only does Advaita-Vedānta take this teaching for granted, but also authors of the Nyāya-Vaiśeṣika school[2] and even Kumārila.[3]

The concept of *jīvanmukti* in the philosophy of Madhva was up to now a matter of contradictory opinions. The main reason for this confusion was the assumption that Madhva nowhere in his works used the *terminus technicus* (*jīvanmukta/ jīvanmukti*) while discussing the teaching of liberation. Many Indologists therefore thought that Madhva rejected the concept of liberation while alive. For instance, Hiriyanna remarks: "Like Rāmānuja, Madhva also rejects the ideal of *jīvanmukti*".[4] Sheridan too opines in his paper that Madhva does not

---

[1] Cf. Sprockhoff 1962; Vetter 1995: 213ff.; 219f. and 225f. See also Slaje 2000: 184n. 8. This widely held doctrine, which (Garbe 1894: 181) described as a "common Indian idea" (= allgemein-indische Idee) is testified to by several single studies, and in particular by two other publications, namely of Fort and Mumme 1996 as well as of Fort 1998.

[2] Cf. Slaje 1986 and Mesquita 1995. *Jīvanmukti* is also accepted in Yogavāsiṣṭha (cf. Slaje 1994: 94f.) as also in Sāṃkhya, Yoga and in the Śaiva schools (cf. Fort and Mumme 1996), as well as Oberhammer (1994: 75ff.).

[3] Cf. Mesquita 1994.

[4] Cf. Hiriyanna 1951: 199. Likewise Puthiadam 1985: 293: "It is true that Madhva does not accept the doctrine of jīvanmukti. But something equivalent is to be found in his teaching." In a similar way, also Radhakrishnan 1929: Vol. I, p. 748; see also Sinha 1952: Vol. II, p. 699. Siauve, who has left several superb studies on Madhva, did not deal explicitly with Madhva's teaching of *jīvanmukti*. It seems that she rejected it, basing herself on the opinion of Jayatīrtha (Siauve 1957: 51): "... l'illumination précède la délivrance et il est dit qu' entre ces deux moments la vie du *jīvanmukta*, du délivré vivant, continue sous l'effet de l'impulsion du *karman*, de la force des actes passés, jusqu'au moment où le stock du *prārabdhakarman* est épuisé. Cette assertion est absurde, réplique Jayatīrtha: *acetanānāṃ karmaṇāṃ svatantrabhagavatprasādapratibandhakatvāyogāt* (N.S. 68a, 1-2) 'parce qu'il ne

use the technical term: "It is true that the term *jīvanmukti* is not found in the writings [of Madhva]."[5]

In contrast to the Indologists named here, Sheridan is however of the opinion that "the concept of 'liberation while living' ... is quite compatible with Madhva's teaching"[6] and he moreover, attempts to show that "Madhva's teaching of *aparokṣajñāna*, the immediate knowledge of God, is functionally equivalent to Advaita Vedānta's teaching of *jīvanmukti*".[7]

This rather cautious opinion of Sheridan[8] however is in open contradiction to the clear statements of Madhva which so far were unknown to the Indologists on account of which they could not be used to work out in detail Madhva's teaching of *jīvanmukti*. In the following, new materials on the subject matter will be presented and discussed, taking into account Madhva's unknown sources which he cites as a supporting evidence for his teaching of *jīvanmukti*.[9]

The starting point of the following discussion is an unknown quote, which Madhva ascribes to a well known

---

se peut que des [résidus] inconscients d'actes aient capacité de faire obstacle à la grâce du Bienheureux qui est libre' ... Pourtant les dvaitin reconnaissent bien eux-mêmes un délai entre la vision, (*aparokṣa-jñāna*) et la délivrance finale, mais cela ne tient pas au *prārabdha-karman* et cela ne met pas en cause l'unique causalité du Seigneur: *vastutas tu bhagavān evānāder api bandhasya nivartaka iti sādhūktam* (N.S. 68a, 4) 'mais en réalité il est exact de dire que c'est le Bienheureux qui peut supprimer ce lien, bien qu'il soit sans commencement'"; cf. Siauve 1968: 269; see also below n. 90.

[5] Cf. Sheridan 1996: 91. However, he mentions the reason why Madhva avoided the technical term, when he remarks (p. 94): "In the fourteenth century Madhva would not have used the term without seeming to agree with the Advaitin concept of liberation ...".

[6] Ibidem.

[7] Ibidem.

[8] Sheridan frequently speaks of "functional similarity" or that "the term *jīvanmukti* ... was later equated with his teaching of *aparokṣa-jñāna* by his commentator Vyāsatīrtha (1460-1539)" (see Sheridan 1996: 94; 107). Dasgupta (1975: Vol. IV, p. 88) too is cautious in his statement regarding this teaching: "... Thus Madhva favours the doctrine of jīvanmukti."

[9] Special inquiries into the unknown literary sources of Madhva have been carried out by me in Mesquita 2000_1 [= 1997].

source while commenting on BhāgP IV 4,20[10]. As a matter of fact, this quote not only mentions the *terminus technicus* for liberation while alive[11] but also gives its precise definition. The śloka above referred to runs as follows:

karmapravṛttaṃ ca nivṛttam apy uta
vede vivicyobhayaliṅgam āśritam /
virodhi tad yaugapadaikakartari
dvayaṃ tathābrahmaṇi karma na rcchati //

Taking into consideration the textual changes Madhva introduces (he reads *uta* instead of *ṛtam* and *tathā ābrahmaṇi* instead of *tathā brahmaṇi*) we could translate the śloka as follows:

"Since the religious rite in the Veda is differentiated either as performed (with the expectation of wordly or otherwordly reward) or as performed [without that ex-

---

[10] BhāgTN p. 280,10f.; cf. also BhāgP IV 29,13 and VII 15,47; MS XII 89-90 and KūrmaP I 2,63f.; below n. 28.

[11] This term is also referred to elsewhere, e.g. in AiUBh (p.209,8f.) along with *videhamukti*; BSūBh p. 198,25f. In some other unknown quotations Madhva mentions this teaching with equivalent wordings, as in Anuv p. 187,13-15: *muktiś ca dvividhā tatra sukhaṃ nityaṃ tathāparam ... iti paiṅgi-śruter*; BhāgTN p. 51,10-11:

jñānādivyaktir avyaktiḥ sukhaduḥkhādikaṃ tathā /
sudṛṣṭabrahmatattvānāṃ bhavaty ārabdhakarmaṇā /
iti brahmavaivarte;

ibid. p. 266,8-9:

tattvajñānaṃ tu devānāṃ garbhasthānāṃ bhaviṣyati /
uttamānām ṛṣīṇāṃ vāpy anyeṣāṃ bahujanmagam /
...iti skānde;

ibid. p. 272,3-5: ... *iti harivaṃśeṣu*; ibid. p. 352,1-2. ... *iti harivaṃśeṣu.*
GīBh p. 4,29-30:

yas tv evātmarato muktaḥ kāryaṃ tasyaiva nāsti hi /
tasmāt kurv eva karmāṇīty āha kṛṣṇo 'rjunaṃ smayam /
... iti skānde;

see also below n. 15, 58, 66, 67, 68, 76, 87 and 89.

pectation],[12] it follows [that the religious rite] has a double mark. When this rite [with double mark] is performed simultaneously by one and the same agent, it is contradictory. Surely, this kind of religious rite with double mark is not [performed by an agent with an immediate and direct knowledge] which includes Brahman."

In the following commentary of Madhva – re-wording the passage as *ābrahmaṇi samyagjñānini* – the meaning is quite clear: Madhva understands the above śloka in the sense of liberation while alive. He supports his interpretation with an unknown quote from Bhaviṣyatpurāṇa:

ābrahmā sthitadhīr jīvanmuktaś cety abhidhīyate /
yas tasya na nivṛttaṃ ca pravṛttaṃ karma ceṣyate /
yat tu devāḥ prakurvanti sa mahāniyamaḥ smṛtaḥ /
svargādyarthaṃ pravṛttaṃ syān nivṛttaṃ muktaye tu yat /
sa mahāniyamo nāma karma yat tv ādhikārikam /
mahato niyamād viṣṇoḥ prī tyā muktau sukhonnatiḥ /
kecin nivṛttam ity āhur mahāniyamam apy uta /
iti bhaviṣyatpurāṇe.

"A sage firm in judgement and wisdom, having [immediate and direct knowledge] of Brahman, and who is called *jīvanmukta*, does not perform a religious rite [with the expectation of wordly or otherwordly reward and at the same time a rite] that is not connected with it. However, that which the deities perform is declared as a 'great vow'. [A religious rite] which is performed for the sake of heaven, etc. is [a rite, which is connected with the expectation of otherworldly] reward, while [the rite] performed for the sake of liberation is not connected with [worldly or otherworldly reward]. This 'great vow' is namely a supreme performance. Because of this 'great

[12] In MBh (XII 327,61f.) the view of *pravṛtta* and *nivṛtta* is handed down as the teaching of Kapila; cf. Bronkhorst 1998: 75f.; see also GīBh p. 27,3f. *ad* Gī II 47 and GīBhŚ, below n. 17.

vow' [and] because of the affection of Viṣṇu, an increase of happiness takes place in liberation. Some learned people declare that [a religious rite performed without the expectation of worldly or otherworldly reward] is also a 'great vow'." So runs the Bhaviṣyatpurāṇa.

A careful examination of the structure of this passage reveals traces of a ficticious source, as I have discussed in detail elsewhere.[13] First of all, the passage is intimately associated with the previous statement of Madhva and it is in complete harmony with it. Furthermore, it is not traceable, although it is attributed to a well known Purāṇa. In addition, the quote touches upon a new subject which is not mentioned in the śloka of BhāgP and also in the short paraphrase of it by Madhva, namely the behaviour of the deities as an example for the human beings. The deities do not act for the sake of a worldly or otherworldly reward. For this reason, their behaviour is praised as a 'great vow'. In this connection an opinion of some learned people is referred to, namely that selfless action of human beings too is praiseworthy and therefore a 'great vow'. We have here a quote within a quotation. It is interesting that Madhva cites in this connection another untraceable quote, again from the Purāṇa-literature:

yadi devāś ca ṛṣyādyā nindyante yatra kutracit /
na tāvatā guṇair hīnāḥ sthitaprajñā hi te matāḥ /
yathāyogyaṃ tu tātparyaṃ nindāyām anyad eva tu /
iti gāruḍe.

"When the deities and Ṛṣis are sometimes reproached, it does not mean that they are deprived of their good qualities [according to their intrinsic aptitudes].[14] For they are taken as [liberated], as being firm in judgement and wisdom. In the reproach another special sense is expressed

[13] Cf. Mesquita 2000_1: 19f.; 91f.; 126f. [=1997: 16f.; 72f.; 101f.]
[14] Cf. Mesquita 2000: 506n. 663.

[which is not based on hate or jealousy].” This is said in the Garuḍapurāṇa.[15]

With this quote, Madhva closes his commentary on BhāgP IV 4,20. Some new aspects on the liberation are also put forward in this context, which have no reference to the śloka that is commented upon. But Madhva explains this point in another work of his, the Anuvyākhyāna[16] in an independent way, that is to say, without quoting sources:

vikarmalepo naivāsti samyagdṛṣṭimatāṃ kvacit /
guṇahāniś ca naivāsti brahmaṇas tv avikarmataḥ //

---

[15] In BSūBh pp. 226,19-227,9 Madhva puts foward another untraceable quote which he attributes to the same Purāṇa. All the different types of liberation are mentioned and explained therein, starting with the liberation while alive, however without the *terminus technicus*: ... *kecid* atraiva *mucyante notkrāmanti kadācana*, followed by Kramamukti and Videhamukti: *gāruḍe ca* –

ātmety eva paraṃ devam upāsya harim avyayam /
kecid atraiva *mucyante notkrāmanti kadācana /*
atraiva ca sthitis teṣām ...

Likewise also in GīT p. 160,20-23: ... *aparokṣadṛśo viṣṇoḥ* śarīre 'pi sataḥ *purā* ... *iti mahāvarāhe*; cf. another untraceable quotation to the point in GīBh pp. 35,12-14:

sthitaprajño 'pi yas tūrdhvaḥ prāpya raudraṃ padaṃ tataḥ /
sāṅkarṣaṇaṃ tato muktim agād viṣṇuprasādataḥ /
iti gāruḍe;

also ibid. 29,17-18 and from *vāyupurāṇa* in BSūBh p. 158,12-14 also ibid. 221,12-14: *bhaviṣyatpurāṇe ca* ... and also from *brahmāṇḍapurāṇa* in AiUBh p. 220,19-22, see also below n. 18. Bos [1983: 165 n. 3] asserts that Śaṅkara nowhere in his works did use the technical term *jīvanmukti* but only its descriptions which come close to the actual word and that the term has been employed only in the later tradition. As a matter of fact, Śaṅkara did use this term once and explained its meaning in his GīBh (*ad* VI 27): (praśāntamanasam) *prakarṣeṇa śāntaṃ mano yasya saḥ praśāntamanaḥ taṃ praśāntamanasaṃ* (hy enaṃ yoginaṃ sukhaṃ uttamam) *niratiśayaṃ* (upaity) *upagacchati* (śāntarajasam) *prakṣīṇamohādikleśarajasam ityarthaḥ* (brahmabhūtam) *jīvanmuktaṃ brahmaiva sarvam ity evaṃ niścayavantaṃ* (brahmabhūtaṃ akalmaṣam) *dharmādharmādivarjitam.*

[16] Anuv p. 173,15; cf. below n. 87; SŚS 19cd; see also GīBhŚ *ad* XIII 13: *uttarapakṣa.*

Both the above quotes of Madhva, although different in their structure, still pursue the same aim, in the sense that they confirm the principal statement of the discussion, namely, that the only way to overcome the mundane existence or bondage (*saṃsāra*) and to achieve liberation is the *nivṛttaṃ karma*, an action performed without the expectation of worldly or other-worldly reward, since its opposite the *pravṛttaṃ karma* produces new *karma*, which binds human beings to the mundane existence, undergoing transmigration (*abandhakatvaṃ tv akāmena bhavati*).[17]

And the stage of absence of worldly desires or passions (*vairāgya*) which is free of *pravṛttaṃ karma* is achieved through yogic practices which keep the senses under control, leading finally to *samādhi*. The two Purāṇas quoted above point to this path of Yoga when they define the Jīvanmukta as *sthitadhī* or *sthitaprajña*.[18] This is definitely stated with a clear reference to Gī (II 51f.):

---

[17] Cf. GīBh p. 39,13. This is a very important topos in the doctrine of liberation, which is very common in the philosophy of other Indian authors such as Śrīdhara (= Mesquita 1995: 235f.: *lābhapūjādiprayojanam anabhisandhāya* ...); Kumārila (= Mesquita 1994: 458f.) and Śaṅkara: *pravṛttiḥ pravartanaṃ bandhahetuḥ karmamārgaḥ śāstravihitaviṣayaḥ ... nivṛttir mokṣahetuḥ saṃnyāsamārgaḥ ... pravṛttinivṛttī karmasaṃnyāsamārgāv ity avagamyate* (GīBhŚ *ad* XVIII 30; see also Bos 1983: 170f. and Oberhammer 1994: 18f.). This opinion is advocated also in Yogavāsiṣṭha (Slaje 2000: 174f.), however, with a striking difference. *Vairāgya* is not considered as a means of liberation, but as a goal (Slaje 2000: 180).

[18] Cf. BSūBh p. 158,12-14: *vāyuprokte* (untraceable)

> *sthitaprajñatvam āptā ye jñānena paramātmanaḥ* /
> *brahmalokaṃ gatāḥ sarve brahmaṇā ca paraṃ gatāḥ* /
> *tīrṇatartavyabhāgāś ca svecchayopāsate param* / iti.

The term *sthitaprajña* is also used by Advaitins as a distinguishing mark of a *jīvanmukta*, e.g. Śaṅkara: *sthitaprajñalakṣaṇāni* (Bos 1983: 168f.); Vimuktātman: ... *ityādīni jīvanmuktivacanāni sthitaprajñāguṇātītalakṣaṇavacanāni copapannārthāni bhavanti* (IS p. 77,13-15) and Citsukha in Citsukhī (CS p. 609,6f.) also the late Advaitin Vidyāraṇya (cf. Sprockhoff 1970: 137). Maṇḍanamiśra is the only advaitin, who understands *sthitaprajña*, not as a *siddha* (= *jīvanmukta*) but as a *sādhaka* (BS p. 130,19-21). Citsukha refuted this view in his Citsukhī (o.c.). Sarvajñātman – who first supported the doctrine of *jīvanmukti* – gave it up in favour of *sadyomukti* (cf. Mesquita 2000: 181n. 375).

karmajaṃ buddhiyuktā hi phalaṃ tyaktvā manīṣiṇaḥ /
janmabandhavinirmuktāḥ padaṃ gacchanty anāmayam //

It is therefore not purely coincidental that Madhva replaces in GīBh the Pratīka *buddhiyuktāḥ* with *samyagjñāninaḥ*[19], a description he used above to define a liberated while still living, while commenting on BhāgP IV 4,20. In full agreement with it, Gī II 54-56[20] mentions other marks of a liberated while still living, as *sthitadhī, sthitaprajña, samādhisthita.* Madhva comments upon it in GīBh as follows:

> *na hi samādhiṃ kurvatas tasya śubhāśubhaprāptir asti / asaṃprajñātasamādheḥ / saṃprajñāte tv avirodhaḥ / tathāpi na tatraiveti niyamaḥ /*
> *kāmādayo na jāyante hy api vikṣiptacetasām /*
> *jñānināṃ jñānanirdhūtamalānāṃ devasaṃśrayāt /*
> iti smṛteḥ.[21]
>
> Indeed a person who is deeply absorbed in meditation does not experience either [worldly] happiness or unhappiness since he is in a state of unconsciousness. However, [this statement] is not incompatible with meditation in the state of consciousness. Even [in the meditation with consciousness] there is no [worldly happiness or unhappiness]. This is the rule on account of [the following statement of the] sacred tradition [untraceable]: "A person having a higher knowledge [and therefore,] not being in the state of consciousness, whose impurities

---

[19] GīBh p. 29,31-32: *buddhiyuktāḥ samyagjñānino bhūtvā padaṃ gacchanti / sayogakarma jñānasādhanam / tan mokṣasādhanam iti bhāvaḥ.*

[20] Gī II 54-56: *arjuna uvāca –*
sthitaprajñasya kā bhāṣā samādhisthitasya keśava /
sthitadhīḥ kiṃ prabhāṣeta kim āsīta vrajeta kim //54 //
śrībhagavān uvāca –
prajahāti yadā kāmān sarvān pārtha manogatān /
ātmany evātmanā tuṣṭaḥ sthitaprajñas tadocyate /
duḥkheṣv anudvignamanā sukheṣu vigataspṛhaḥ /
vītarāgabhayakrodhaḥ sthitadhīr munir ucyate //56 //

[21] Cf. Cf. GīBh p. 31,21-24.

have been annihilated by [this] knowledge [causing release], has no objects of pleasure, etc, since he is taking refuge in God [Viṣṇu]."

In his commentary of Gī III 17 we find exactly the same ideas, which Madhva wraps up in an untraceable quotation:

> *ātmaratir evety* (= Gī III 17) *avadhāraṇād asaṃprajñātasamādhisthasyaiva kāryaṃ na vidyate /*
> *sthitaprajñasyāpi kāryo dehādir dṛśyate yadā /*
> *svadharmo*[22] *mama tuṣṭyarthaḥ sā hi sarvair apekṣitā /*
> iti vacanāc ca pañcarātre.

> On account of the statement *ātmaratir eva* one who is engaged in meditation, without being in the state of consciousness, is not obliged to perform a religious rite because of the [following] instruction in the Pañcarātra-[saṃhitā]: "Even one who is firm in judgement and wisdom [i. e. one who is *jīvanmukta*] has to perform the religious rite, when his body etc. is visible (= *saṃprajñātasamādhi*). The aim [of practising] his own duty is my (= Viṣṇu's) satisfaction. For this is desired by all [my devotees]."

Madhva's remarks in connection with Gī VI 3 are in complete agreement with this teaching, for instance, when he discusses the question how long one has to practise the religious rites (*kiyatkālaṃ karma kartavyam*). His answer is: one should practise the religious rites until he has won the immediate and direct knowledge, and with it the liberation while alive, and even beyond that.[23] Exactly in this sense Madhva renders also

---

[22] Cf, GīT p. 1,20: *bhaktyā bhagavadārādhanam eva paramadharmas tadviruddhaḥ sarvo 'py adharmaḥ*; ibid. p.2,13: ... *ityādinā svadharmeṇa bhagavadārādhanasyaiva kartavyatvaṃ tadanyasya tyājyatvaṃ ca.*

[23] Cf. BSūBh p. 197,24-26:

> *śṛṇuyād yāvad ajñānaṃ matir yāvad ayuktatā /*
> *dhyānaṃ ca yāvad īkṣā syān nekṣā kvacana bādhyate /*
> *dṛṣṭatattvasya ca dhyānaṃ yadā dṛṣṭir na vidyate /*
> *bhaktiś cānantakālīnā parame brahmaṇi sphuṭā /*

the Pratīka *yogārūḍhasya* as *apararokṣajñāninaḥ*. This situation in the life of a *jīvanmukta* implies both the states, namely that of *asaṃprajñatasamādhi* and *saṃprajñātasamādhi*.[24] Whereas in the state of *asaṃprajñātasamādhi* all wordly activities calm down, since the *jīvanmukta* loses his individual consciousness,[25] the *jīvanmukta* remains in the state of *saṃprajñātasamādhi* practising devotional works, even when he comes across distress.[26] Here too, Madhva emphasizes his explanation with the help of an untraceable quote:

> *aparokṣajñānino 'pi samādhyādiphalam uktam / tasya sarvopaśamena samādhir eva kāraṇaṃ prādhānyenety arthaḥ / tathāpi yadā bhoktavyoparamas tadaiva samyag asaṃprajñātasamādhir jāyate / anyadā tu bhagavaccaritādau sthitiḥ / tac coktam –*
> *ye tvāṃ paśyanti bhagavaṃs ta eva sukhinaḥ param /*
> *teṣāṃ eva ca samyak tu samādhir jāyate nṛṇām /*
> *bhoktavyakarmaṇy akṣīṇe japena kathayāpi vā /*
> *vartayanti mahātmānas tvadbhāktās tvatparāyaṇaḥ / iti.*

The yogic practices or works produce a firm judgement and wisdom (*sthitadhī, sthitaprajñā*) and this makes possible a correct execution of religious rites within the meaning of *nivṛttaṃ karma*. According to different expressions of Madhva, it fol-

---

> *ā vimukter vidhir nityaṃ svata eva tataḥ param /*
> *iti brahmāṇḍe* (untraceable);

see also Mesquita 1994: 469n. 89; Mesquita 1995: 226 and 242n. 104.

[24] Cf. NyāV p. 220,22-23: *svena rūpeṇābhiniṣpadyata iti muktasya spaṣṭaṃ pratibhātatvāc chrutam* (ChU VIII 3.4) and BSūBh p. 220,4-6; see also Śrīdhara (cf. Mesquita 1995: 241f.) and Kumārila (Mesquita 1994: 471f.).

[25] Cf. Anuv p. 153,18:

> *śravaṇādi vinā naiva kṣaṇaṃ tiṣṭhed api kvacit /*
> *atyaśakye tu nidrādau punar eva samācaret /*

see also GīBh p. 4,29-30: ... *iti skānde* and NK p. 687,15f.: ... *ātmatattvajñānam eva kevalaṃ tadānīṃ saṃjāyate na bahiḥsaṃvedanam / bāhyendriyavyāpāroparamāt*; see above n. 24.

[26] Cf. SŚS 21: ... *nityam upāsanaṃ kāryam āpady api brahma tena yāty aparokṣatām.*

lows that he has in view primarily the pious works of Bhakti.[27] Madhva elaborates this point later in GīBh again with the help of untraceable quotes:

tasmāj jñāninām karmāpy anuṣṭheyaṃ / karmiṇām api gṛhasthānāṃ jñātavyo bhagavān / na hi jñānaṃ vinā karmaṇaḥ samyaganuṣṭhānaṃ bhavati /
niṣkāmaṃ jñānapūrvaṃ ca nivṛttam iha cocyate /
nivṛttaṃ sevamānas tu brahmābhyeti sanātanam /
buddhyāvihiṃsan puṣpair vā praṇavena samarcayet /
vāsudevātmakaṃ brahma mūlamantreṇa vā yatiḥ /
muktir astīti niyamo brahmadṛg yasya vidyate /
tasyāpy ānandavṛddhiḥ syād vaiṣṇavaṃ karma kurvataḥ /
karma brahmadṛśā hīnaṃ na mukhyam iti kīrtitam /
tasmāt karmeti tat prāhur yat kṛtaṃ brahmadarśinā /
etasmān nyāsināṃ lokam saṃyānti gṛhiṇo 'pi hi /
jñānamārgaḥ karmamārga iti bhedas tato na hi /
tasmād āśramabhedo 'yaṃ karmasaṃkocasaṃbhavaḥ /
iti vyāsasmṛteḥ /
mokṣopāyo yoga iti tadrūpo nyāsa eva tu /
viṣṇvarpitatayā bhadro nānyo nyāsaḥ kathaṃcana /
iti āgneye.[28]

---

[27] Cf. also BhāgTN p. 4,16: *dharma iti projjhitakaitavo 'phalāpekṣayā / īśvarārpeṇa paramaḥ*; see also above n. 22. and Śaṅkara, GīBhŚ (*upodghāta*): ... *īśvarārpaṇabuddhyānuṣṭhīyamānaḥ sattvaśuddhaye bhavati phalābhisandhivarjitaḥ*; ib. *ad* V 11.

[28] GīT p.59,20-29; cf. also MuUBh p. 492,22-23 and GīBh p. 27,12 as well as p. 39,15f. The first śloka is quoted here as belonging to Manusmṛti, in BhāgTN p. 660,5-6 however, as a quote from Mahābhārata. The genuine quote from the Manusmṛti (XII 89-90) runs as follows:

iha cāmutra vā kāmyaṃ pravṛttaṃ karma kīrtyate /
niṣkāmaṃ jñānapūrvaṃ tu nivṛttaṃ upadiśyate //
pravṛttam karma saṃsevya devānām eti sāmyatām /
nivṛttaṃ sevamānas tu bhūtāny eti pañca vai //

cf. also KūrmaP I 2,63f.:

tasmāj jñānena sahitaṃ karmayogaṃ samāśrayet /
pravṛttaṃ ca nivṛttaṃ dvividhaṃ karma vaidikam //
jñānapūrvaṃ nivṛttaṃ syāt pravṛttaṃ yad ato 'nyathā /
nivṛttaṃ sevamānas tu yāti tat paramaṃ padam //
tasmān nivṛttaṃ saṃsevyam anyathā saṃsaret punaḥ / ...

Therefore, those endowed with higher knowledge should also perform religious rites. In the same way, householders should perform religious rites, they should inquire after the divine [Viṣṇu]. For without the higher knowledge [of Viṣṇu] the proper performance of the religious rites is not possible according to the teaching of Vyāsasmṛti: "A disinterested/unselfish [religious rite] which is based on a higher knowledge is called here [a religious rite], which is not connected with the expectation [of worldly or otherworldly] reward. One who practises [religious rites], however, without being connected with reward, reaches the eternal Brahman.
An ascetic should worship Brahman in the manifestation of Vāsudeva[29] either with mental perception, or with flowers without harming them, or with the primary sacred formula Om. [A devotee] who is in possession of Brahma-vision and of the certainty that he is released, experiences an increase of happiness, insofar as he performs Vaiṣṇava religious rites. A religious rite without Brahma-vision is not called an essential rite. Therefore, [the sages] teach that the religious rites performed by [devotees] in possession of Brahma-vision is an essential rite (*mukhya* = *mahāniyama*).[30] For this reason the householders too go to the heaven of ascetics (*saṃnyāsin*) (that means that the householders become equal to saṃnyāsins). Therefore, there exists no difference between *jñānamārga* and *karmamārga*. Accordingly, the distinction between the [four different] stages of life constrains [the meaning of the term] *karman* [since *nivṛttam karma* is not a distinguishing mark of a Saṃnyāsin]."[31]

---

[29] Madhva seems to follow here a particular teaching of Pañcarātra. According to it, God Viṣṇu takes outward appeareances of four Vyūhas as Vāsudeva, Saṃkarṣaṇa, Pradyumna and Aniruddha in order to be available for the devotees as objects of worship in the ritual; cf. Oberhammer 1971: 49.
[30] Cf. above p. 3.
[31] Cf. also GīBh p. 39,17f.: *saṃnyāsaḥ kāmyakarmaparityāgaḥ ... viraktānāṃ eva ca jñānam uktam ... ato na karmatyāga eva mokṣasādhanam / yatyāśramas tu prāyatyārtho bhagavattoṣārthaś ca / aprayatatvam eva hi prāyo gṛha-*

In AgniP it is said: "Yoga is the means of release. Renunciation is indeed its outward appearance. There is no other auspicious renunciation whatsoever since it is granted by Viṣṇu."

Both sources quoted here are also untraceable. Only the first śloka in the quotation of Vyāsasmṛti, which Madhva attributes elsewhere to different sources, has most likely similarities with the Śloka in KūrmaP. It is, however, strange that Madhva does not adduce it as instance in this connection.[32]

It is remarkable that the contents of the first quote, namely from Vyāsasmṛti fits in exactly with the subject area of another untraceable quote from Bhaviṣyatpurāṇa in BhāgP, namely *nivṛttaṃ karma.* Exactly as in BhāgTN (*viṣṇoḥ prītyā muktau sukhonnatiḥ*), here also, the Vedic religious rites are intimately connected with Vaiṣṇava religious rites and Bhakti. All these rites bring about an increase of happiness (*ānandavṛddhiḥ syād vaiṣṇavaṃ karma kurvataḥ*). *ābrahmā sthitadhīḥ* or *ābrahman samyagjñānin* in BhāgTN is in the quote of *vyāsasmṛti* replaced by *brahmadṛk.* There is also an agreement with the definition of *nivṛttam karma* in Bhaviṣyatpurāṇa, as *mahāniyama.* It is said to be the teaching of some sages: *kecin nivṛttaṃ karma iti mahāniyamam.* In the Vyāsasmṛti also, a similar statement is made and reported as the opinion of some sages: *tasmāt karmeti tat prāhur yat kṛtaṃ brahmadarśinā.* However, there is also an addition, namely the role of the four different stages of life as well as the preponderance of *saṃnyāsin* are strongly played down.[33] In the same manner, also the role of religious rites as means of release (*karmamārga*), inasfar as they cannot operate independently of *jñānamārga* are therefore to be subsumed under the latter. In GīBh *ad* III 32

---

sthādīnām / itarakarmodyogāt / aprayatānāṃ ca na jñānam (see also below n. 43); Śaṅkara: *nivṛttir mokṣahetuḥ saṃnyāsamārgaḥ* (cf. above n. 17).

[32] Cf. above nn. 17 and 28.

[33] Cf. above nn. 30-31 where Madhva criticizes the traditional understanding of Saṃnyāsin. We find similar limitations also in Yogavāsiṣṭha and in the works of Abhinavagupta, cf. Slaje 2000: 180n. 87.

Madhva supplements this reasoning by differentiating religious rites without the expectation of reward (*nivṛttaṃ karma*) from the immediate knowledge (*aparokṣajñāna*). The religious rites mentioned above are made subservient to the immediate knowledge since they are merely means for the purification of mind:

> *akāmakarmaṇāṃ antaḥkaranaśuddhidvārā jñānān mokṣo bhavati* | *tac coktam –*
> *karmabhiḥ śuddhasattvasya vairāgyaṃ jāyate hṛdi* |
> iti bhāgavate | (untraceable) *viraktānām eva ca jñānam ity uktam.*[34]

Madhva supports this argument again with the help of another untraceable quote that the immediate knowledge (*aparokṣajñāna*) is the only means of release:

> *ye tv evaṃ nivṛttakarmiṇas te 'pi mucyante jñānadvāra* |
> *kimv aparokṣajñāninaḥ* | *na tu sādhanāntaram ucyate –*
> *nivṛttādīni karmāṇi hy aparokṣeśadṛṣṭaye* |
> *aparokṣeśadṛṣṭis tu muktau kiṃcin na mārgate* |
> *sarvaṃ tad antarādhāya muktaye sādhanaṃ bhavet* |
> *na kiṃcid antarādhāya nirvāṇāyāparokṣadṛk* |
> *iti hy uktaṃ nārāyaṇāṣṭākṣarakalpe.*

> Those who perform religious rites without the expectation of reward are also released by means of knowledge. How much more those who possess immediate knowledge? No other useful means is mentioned [in this connection]. For, it has been handed down in Nārāyaṇāṣṭākṣarakalpa: "Indeed religious rites without expectation of reward are fit for immediate knowledge of Lord Viṣṇu. The direct knowledge of Lord Viṣṇu, however, does not seek something else for the sake of release [since it is identical with the release]. All useful means, inasmuch as they comprise [the immediate knowledge of

---

[34] GīBh p. 39,18-19; cf. above n.31; SŚS 15cd; above n. 27.

Viṣṇu] would lead to release. The immediate knowledge – inasmuch as it comprises nothing – points towards release."[35]

The foremost consequence of this point of view, is that Madhva firmly rejects the view of Vedānta authors as well as of Kumārila and Śrīdhara etc.[36] regarding the *jñānakarmasamuccayavāda*: *ata eva samuccayaniyamo 'pi nirākṛtaḥ.* It is therefore, an established fact that Madhva himself was the first to relate the teaching of *aparokṣajñāna* to *jīvanmukti*, and not Vyāsatīrtha, who lived in the 16th century.[37]

It is quite interesting to see that Madhva's description of release as 'the direct vision of Lord' is in accordance with the teaching of the theistic authors before him, as Śrīdhara and Bhāsarvajña.[38] And this implies that it is not required at all to assert that Madhva borrowed his teaching of *jīvanmukti* from a *māyāvādin* like Śaṅkara.[39] And this point is strongly supported by the fact that Madhva seems to follow Śrīdhara when he describes the role of the religious rites, performed without the expectation of reward in the process of release. Śrīdhara attaches great importance to the teaching that the aim of religious rites is to destroy the sins (*pratyavāyanirodhārthaṃ vihitāni anuṣṭheyāni*).[40]Madhva gives his own view on this matter, when he comments Gī III 20:

---

[35] GīBh p. 46,10f.

[36] Cf. NK p. 683,11f.: *kiṃ jñānamātrān muktiḥ / uta jñānakarmasamuccayāt / jñānakarmasamuccayād iti vadamaḥ.*

[37] Cf. Sheridan 1996: 94; 107; see above n. 8.

[38] Cf. NK, *maṅgala*-Vers:

dhyānaikatānamanaso vigatapracārāḥ
paśyanti yaṃ kam api nirmalam advitīyam /
jñānātmane vighaṭitākhilabandhanāya
tasmai namo bhagavate puruṣottamāya //

and NyāBh p. 590,7-8; *tataḥ samādhiprakarṣātiśayaprāptāv acireṇaiva kālena bhagavantam anaupamyasvabhāvaṃ śivam avithataṃ pratyakṣataḥ paśyati*; see also Mesquita 1995: 217f.

[39] Cf. Sheridhan 1996: 94.

[40] Cf. Mesquita 1995: 226n. 42. Kumārila too follows this teaching, cf. Mesquita 1994: 469n. 91. This opinion is very common in the Purāṇic and

yatra ca tīrthādy eva muktisādhanam ucyate –
brahmajñānena vā muktiḥ prayāgamaraṇena vā /
athavā snānamātreṇa gomatyāḥ kṛṣṇasannidhau /
ityādau tatra pāpādimuktiḥ / stutiparatā ca / tatrāpi hi kutracid brahmajñānasādhanatvam evocyate 'nyathā muktiṃ niṣidhya –
brahmajñānaṃ vinā muktir na kathaṃcid apīṣyate /
prayāgādes tu yā muktir jñānopāyatvam eva hi /
ityādau ... yathāha bhagavān –
yāni tīrthādivākyāni karmādiviṣayāṇi ca /
stāvakāny eva tāni syur ajñānāṃ mohakāni vā /
bhaven mokṣas tu maddṛṣṭer nānyatas tu kathaṃcana /
iti nāradīye / ato 'parokṣajñānād eva mokṣaḥ / karma tu tatsādhanam eva.

[By statements] such as: "Release takes place on account of Brahma-knowledge or by death in *prayāga* or merely by taking a bath in the [river] Gomatī in the presence of Kṛṣṇa", is [either] taught that only the places of pilgrimage on the banks of the sacred streams etc. are means of release, in which case, a deliverance from sins is asserted, or [these statements] are made for the sake of eulogizing [the places of pilgrimage]. All such statements declare that only the Brahma-knowledge is the means [of release], denying [at the same time with other declarations like:] "In no case is a release prescribed without the Brahma-knowledge, since the release [which is recommended] because of *prayāga*, etc. serves only as an expedient by means of which one attains the Brahma-knowledge" – that the release takes place in any other wise. In this sense, Lord Viṣṇu proclaimed in the NāradīyaP: "The statements regarding places of pilgrimage, etc. and those with reference to religious rites, etc. could be merely for the sake of extolling them or for the sake of bewilderment of the ignorants. However, release takes

---

Epic literature, cf. MatsyaP XXII 8,13 and 31f.; see also MBh XIII, Appendix 15, 3091f.

place solely through my vision, and never otherwise." For this reason, release comes into being only because of immediate knowledge; religious rite is merely a means to it.

An analysis of these assertions shows that Madhva, like Śrīdhara, considers that the fulfilment of religious rites is an expedient which leads to freedom from sins (*pāpādimukti*). However, unlike Śrīdhara, Madhva is of the opinion that such performance produces also ultimate knowledge (*karma tu tat-sādhanam eva = nivṛttādīni karmāṇi hy aparokṣeṣadṛṣṭaye*).[41] Thus, correct knowledge is a prerequisite for the right performance of religious rites, which in turn brings about an increase of knowledge,[42] leading to final release. Madhva underpins this judgement again with help of an untraceable source in GīT *ad* III 3:

jñānino mokṣaniyamas tathāpi śubhakarmaṇā /
ānandavṛddhir anyena hrāso jñānaṃ tu karmaṇā /
iti paramaśruteḥ.

For, as the *paramaśruti* states: "A person who is in possession of ultimate knowledge is sure of his release. Nevertheless, on account of a good action [, namely a work of vaiṣṇavite devotion] there is an increase in happiness [and] on account of other [evil action] a decrease [in happiness]. [The performance of] religious rites gives rise to ultimate knowledge."

Thus, Madhva emphasizes that the ultimate knowledge is to be achieved only by a person who is active and hard at work. In case the release could be achieved also by persons

---

[41] Cf. above GīBh *ad* III 32; see also above n. 23.

[42] Cf. above n. 28:

niṣkāmaṃ jñānapūrvaṃ ca nivṛttam iha cocyate /
nivṛttaṃ sevamānas tu brahmābhyeti sanātanam /

see also BSūBh (*ad* BSū IV 1,16): *agnihotrādy api mokṣe 'nubhavāyaiva tu-śabdād brahmadarśanavataḥ.*

who are not active, that would imply that even inanimate beings would be released: *jñānam eva tatsādhanaṃ na tu karmākaraṇam ... yadi karmākareṇa muktiḥ syāt sthāvarāṇām / na cākararaṇe karmābhāvān muktir bhavati.*[43]

Activity implies also the use of right means of acquiring release. Madhva follows in this connection the teaching of three stages accepted in the Vedānta and also by other theistic authors,[44] namely *śravaṇa*[45] (Vedic tradition acquired by repeated hearing from Guru's mouth), *manana* (intellectual study) and *nididhyāsanā* (profound and repeated meditation). All these means lead also to direct and ultimate knowledge. Madhva explains this process in his GīBh (*ad* VI 8) as follows:

> *jitātmā hi praśānto bhavati / na tasya manaḥ prāyo viṣayeṣu gacchati / tadā ca paramātmā samyag hṛdy āhitaḥ sannihito bhavati / aparokṣajñānī sa bhavatīty arthaḥ / ... tac coktam –*
> *śravaṇān mananāc caiva yaj jñānam upajāyate /*
> *taj jñānaṃ darśanaṃ viṣṇor vijñānaṃ śaṃbhur abravīt /*
> *... ityādi* (untraceable).[46]

---

[43] Cf. GīBh p. 39,4f. and 17f.; see also above n. 31.

[44] Cf. Mesquita 1995: 233n. 71 and Mesquita 1994: 462; Oberhammer 1984: 86f.

[45] Cf. BSūBh p. 161,22-24:

> *vārāhe ca*:
> *guruprāsado balavān na tasmād balavattaram /*
> *tathāpi śravaṇādiś ca kartavyo mokṣasiddhaye /*
> iti (untraceable);

see also Anuv p. 167,27f.:

> *samyag guruprasādaś ca mukhyato dṛṣṭikāraṇam /*
> *śravaṇādi ca kartavyaṃ nānyathā darśanaṃ kvacit /*
> *guṇādikaṃ guruṃ prāpya taddhīnaṃ nāpnuyāt kvacit ...*

[46] Cf. BSūBh p. 161,5f.: ... *brahmatarke ca* (fictitious source) –

> *śrutvā matvā tathā dhyātvā tadajñānaviparyayau /*
> *saṃśayaṃ ca parāṇudya labhate brahmadarśanam / iti*;

see also Anuv p. 153,14f.:

> *śravaṇaṃ mananaṃ caiva kartavyaṃ sarvathaiva hi /*
> *matiśrutidhyānakālaviśeṣaṃ gurur uttamaḥ /*
> *vetti tasyoktimārgeṇa kurvataḥ syād dhi darśanam / ...* ;

see also above n. 23.

"A self, who has overcome his desires becomes calm. His mind is normally not aimed at the sense-objects. And in this state the supreme Self rests completely in [his] heart [and] is united with him. He is one who possesses an immediate knowledge. This is the meaning" ... It is also said: "The knowledge [of the self] obtained by listening to and intellectual study [of the Vedic scriptures], is the ultimate knowledge; this knowledge is the vision of Viṣṇu, the knowledge of the true nature of God (*vijñāna*), says Śambhu."

It is worth noting that in several untraceable quotes of Madhva, works of devotion are rated higher than the Vedic rites, as in the quote attributed to *Paramaśruti*. In reply to the question raised by one who is qualified to perform Vedic religious works, it is said that he should engage himself in Viṣṇu's worship: *kiṃ mayā kāryam ity eva syād buddhir adhikāriṇaḥ ... upāsanā nityaṃ kartavyeti ādareṇa iti.*[47] Worthy of note is also the statement of Madhva that the aforesaid right means of acquiring immediate knowledge (*aparokṣajñāna*) and release as well as the yogic works are to be subsumed under *upāsanā*:[48]

sopāsanā ca dvividhā śāstrābhyāsasvarūpiṇī /
dhyānarūpā parā caiva tadaṅgaṃ dhāraṇādikam /[49]

Since release is an effect, and since each effect is absolutely dependent on Viṣṇu as *mūlakāraṇa*[50] the *upāsanā* too

[47] Cf. Anuv p. 146,27-28; see also above n. 26 and NyāV p. 207,10-11: *na cānyasyāpi sādhanasya kartuṃ śakyatvān na yāvan muktir dhyānaṃ kāryam iti vācyam / dhyānaṃ vināparokṣajñānākhyaviśeṣakāryānupapatteḥ.*

[48] Bhāsarvajña too develops the notion of *upāsana* in close relation to *dhāraṇā* and sets the conception of *upāsana* above Yoga (cf. Oberhammer 1984: 117ff.). Since Madhva seems to follow Bhāsarvajña in the doctrine of inference (*anumāna*) (cf. Mesquita 2000: 348fn. 291 and 357n. 314) it is possible that he elaborated this concept under the influence of Bhasarvajña; see also the similar doctrine of Maṇḍanamiśra (BS p. 134,1-12) and Śaṅkara (Bos 1983: 171).

[49] Anuv p. 146,29f. For details see Siauve 1968: 262ff.

is not a fruit of human effort,[51] but ultimately an act of mercy, a gift of God Viṣṇu. Madhva ascribes these ideas to a fictitious source *Brahmatarka*:

> *nāhaṃ kartā hariḥ kartā tatpūjā karma cākhilam /*
> *tathāpi matkṛtā pūjā tatprasādena nānyathā /*
> *tadbhaktis tatphalaṃ mahyaṃ tatprasādaḥ punaḥ punaḥ /*
> *karmanyāso harāv evaṃ viṣṇos tṛptikaraḥ sadā /*
> *yasmāt svatantrakartṛtvaṃ viṣṇor eva na cānyagam / ...*
> *iti brahmatarkavacanāt ...*

> "I am not the doer, Hari is the doer. And all [my] religious works are directed towards His worship. Even though this worship is done by me, it is due to his graciousness, not otherwise. Worship of Him [and] its fruit are always in my favour. Entrusting pious works to Hari makes Him always happy, because Viṣṇu alone, and no one else, is the independent doer [of all my works]."[52]

Not only are the *pūjā* and *upāsanā* performed by Viṣṇu's devotees are dependent on Viṣṇu but also the 'vision of Viṣṇu' which results from it; for the *aparokṣajñāna*, by itself, does not yield release. Madhva explains this point as follows:

> *narte tvat kriyate kiṃcid ityāder na hariṃ vinā /*
> *jñānasvabhāvato 'pi syān muktiḥ kasyāpi hi kvacit /*

---

[50] Cf. Mesquita 2000: 470ff. and 497ff.

[51] Cf. BSūBh pp. 5,5 and 138,19: *paramātmāparokṣyaṃ ca tatprasādād eva na jīvaśaktyeti vaktum ucyate,* NyāV p. 127,21-24; Anuv 140,30: *avyakto 'pi svaśaktyaiva bhaktānāṃ dṛśyate hariḥ*; GīBh p. 18,19f.; see also Mesquita 2000: 511ff., in particular p. 516. This was the main reason why, in the later centuries the followers of Madhva rejected the concept of liberation while alive, see above n. 4.

[52] GīT p. 44,28f. Released beings too perform worship of Viṣṇu (BSūBh p. 158,6-8): *brahmatarke ca –*

> *muktā api hi kurvanti svecchayopāsanaṃ hareḥ /*
> *niyamāntaram viprāḥ kuśādyair apy adhīyate /*

see also ibid. p. 143,5-8.

ajñānāṃ jñānado viṣṇur jñānināṃ mokṣadaś ca saḥ /
ānandadaś ca muktāṇāṃ sa evaiko janārdanaḥ /[53]

In this context the concept of Bhakti plays an ambivalent role.[54] Most probably, like Rāmānuja, Madhva understands *bhakti* as *upāsanā.*[55] However, there are passages[56] where Madhva describes *bhakti* as an outcome of knowledge:

jñānapūrvaḥ paraḥ sneho nityo bhaktir itīryate /
ityādivedavacanaṃ sādhanapravidhāyakam //.

Elsewhere, Madhva introduces knowledge as a component of *bhakti* and *bhakti* as a special knowledge:

jñānasya bhaktibhāgatvād bhaktir jñānam itīryate /
jñānasyaiva viśeṣo yad bhaktir ity abhidhīyate //.

Against these interpretations Madhva declares in GīT that *bhakti* is the best or most effective means of release:

---

[53] Anuv p. 2,30f.; ibid. p. 4,21-23:
ato yathārthabandhasya vinā viṣṇuprasādataḥ /
anivṛttes tadarthaṃ hi jijñāsātra vidhīyate /
yathā dṛṣṭyā prasannaḥ san rājā bandhāpanodakṛt /
evaṃ dṛṣṭaḥ sa bhagavān kuryād bandhavibhedanam /

[54] Śrīdhara too, who has adopted several teachings of Yoga (Mesquita 1995: 226ff.) in his doctrine of liberation while alive, uses the concept of Bhakti, most probably in dependence on Yogabhāṣya (*ad* I 23), in order to explain why *ātmajñāna* or *dharma*, an outcome of an intensive meditation upon Vaiśeṣika-categories, cannot bring about release by itself, when it is not supported by the wish of Īśvara (*dharmo'pi tāvan na niḥśreyasaṃ karoti yāvad īśvarecchayā nānugṛhyate*) (Mesquita 1995: 239). Also Bhāsarvajña combines Yoga with *bhakti* in his conception of release (cf. Oberhammer 1984: 312ff.).

[55] ŚBh I, p. 61,1: *dhruvānusmṛtir eva bhaktiśabdenābhidhīyata upāsanaparyāyatvād bhaktiśabdasya / ata eva śrutismṛtibhir evam abhidhīyate ...* Rāmānuja quotes in this connection Gī XI 53-54. Both these ślokas are quoted also by Madhva together with the following remark: *ityādinā viṣṇubhakter eva sarvasādhanottamatvam,* cf. GīT 2,14-16 = Anuv p. 187,29-32.

[56] Cf. Mesquita 2000: 53n. 19.

viṣṇubhakter eva sarvasādhanottamatvaṃ parokṣāparokṣajñānayor jñānino 'pi mokṣasya tadadhīnatvaṃ ca sneho bhaktir iti proktaḥ sarvopāyottamottamaḥ / tenaiva mokṣo nānyena dṛṣṭyādis tasya sādhanam /.[57]

On the other hand, Madhva describes release as a state where a dynamic interaction of knowledge and *bhakti* takes place. They are mutually dependent, inasmuch they complement each other. This is declared in a statement of Madhva in Anuv:

bhaktyā jñānaṃ tato bhaktis tato dṛṣṭis tataś ca sā /
tato muktis tato bhaktiḥ saiva syāt sukharūpiṇī /
bhaktyā prasanno bhagavān dadyāj jñānam anākulam /
tayaiva darśanaṃ yātaḥ pradadyān muktim etayā /.

"Knowledge arises from *bhakti*, and *bhakti* [arises] from it. And vision results from it (*bhakti*). Release is the outcome of *bhakti* and vice versa. It has the nature of bliss. Lord [Viṣṇu] who is kindly disposed by *bhakti* towards [the released] may grant them unconfused knowledge. It is precisely through this [*bhakti* that the released] will have vision [of Viṣṇu]. Because of this [*bhakti* Viṣṇu] will grant release."[58]

---

[57] Cf. MBhTN I 105; Anuv p.187,9f.; GīT pp. 2,16-17 and 4,12-13; cf. also Anuv p. 168,25f. In the Rāmānuja-School, *bhakti* is considered to be special kind of knowledge: *bhaktiś ca jñānaviśeṣa eveti.* Śaṅkara also understands *upāsanā* as *smṛtisantati* and identifies it with *jñāna* (cf. Bos 1983: 171).

[58] Anuv p. 187,28-30 = BSūBh: *māyāvaibhave ca* [unknown source] (see below n. 59); GīT p. 4,8-10:

bhaktyā prasannaḥ paramo dadyāj jñānam anākulam /
bhaktiṃ ca bhūyasīṃ tābhyāṃ prasanno darśanaṃ vrajet /
tato'pi bhūyasīṃ bhaktiṃ dadyāt tābhyāṃ vimocayet /
mukto 'pi tadvaśo nityaṃ bhūyo bhaktisamanvitaḥ /
sādhyānandasvarūpaiva bhaktir naivātra sādhanam / ... ;

NyāV p. 150,21-23: *bhaktyaivainaṃ jānāti bhaktyaivanaṃ paśyati bhaktyaiva bandhād vimucyate bhaktyaivānandībhavati ... bhinatti karmasaṅghātaṃ prasanno bhagavān hariḥ / ityādyāgamāt* (untraceable); BhāgTN p. 272,3-5:

jñānabhaktiṃ vinā naiva muktiḥ kasyāpi vidyate /
tayor ekatareṇaiva viṣṇugenobhayaṃ vinā /

The aforesaid statement implies on the one hand, that release is a state that follows *bhakti* and which has the nature of bliss (*anuvartate ca sā bhaktir muktāv ānandarūpiṇī*) and, on the other hand, the *bhakti* is a way to the release, inasmuch as it consists in the knowledge of Viṣṇu's greatness and might, as such it supposes *bhakti*: *mahatvabuddhir bhaktis tu snehapūrvābhidhīyate.*[59]

The stronger the *bhakti*, the greater the intensity of the bliss in release. We have here an idea of gradation among the released. Madhva ascribes this teaching in GīT to an unknown source (*vacanāc ca*)[60]:

> *yathā bhaktiviśeṣo 'tra dṛśyate puruṣottame /*
> *tathā muktiviśeṣo 'pi jñāninām liṅgabhedane /*

> *evam apy etayor ekabhāve 'nyaniyater dhruvam /*
> *ekenāpi bhaven muktis tadartham tv anyasādhanam /*
> *iti harivaṃśeṣu* (untraceable);

in another untraceable quote (BhāgTN p. 602,7-8) Madhva speaks of three different groups of Bhaktas:

> *kecid unmādavad bhaktā bāhyaliṅgapradarśakāḥ /*
> *kecid āntarabhaktāḥ syuḥ kecic caivobhayātmakāḥ /*
> *mukhaprasādād dārḍhyāc ca bhaktir jñeyā na cānyataḥ /*
> *iti vārāhe.*

[59] BSūBh p. 137,6-7:

> *mahitvabuddhir bhaktis tu snehapūrvābhidhīyate /*
> *tayaiva vyajyate samyag jīvarūpaṃ sukhādikam /*
> *iti pādme* (untraceable).

See also BSūBh p. 168,1-4:

> *māyāvaibhave ca*:
> *bhaktisthaḥ paramo viṣṇus tayaivainaṃ vaśaṃ nayet /*
> *tayaiva darśanaṃ yātaḥ pradadyān muktim etayā /* (= Anuv p. 187,29; cf. n. 58)
> *snehānubandho yas tasmin bahumānapuraḥsaraḥ /*
> *bhaktir iti ucyate saiva karaṇaṃ param īśituḥ /*
> *iti* (untraceable);

ibid. p. 168,2-5: *snehānubandho yas tasmin bahumānapuraḥsaraḥ / bhaktir ity ucyate ...* ; see also MBhTN I 85: *māhātmyajñānapūrvas tu suhṛdaḥ sarvato 'dhikaḥ / sneho bhaktir iti proktaḥ ... iti bhaviṣyatparvavacana* (fictitious quote); ibid. I 105: *jñānapūrvaḥ paraḥ sneho nityo bhaktir itīryate / iti vedavacana* (untraceable).

[60] GīT p. 30,14-16. In BSūBh p. 138,7- 9. Madhva attributes the first śloka to a Smṛti without giving further details; cf. below n. 82, see also Mesquita 2000: 242n. 7 and p. 519f.

yogināṃ bhinnaliṅgānām āvirbhūtasvarūpiṇām /
prāptānāṃ paramānandaṃ tāratamyaṃ sadaiva hi / iti

The fact that there are different degrees of knowledge and *bhakti* among the devotees who follow the path of yoga for the sake of release is determined by the karmic residues of every individual soul, and not by its intrinsic aptitude (*yogyatā*).[61] In this sense, the karmic residues have a considerable influence on the process of release, inasmuch as the duration of the total destruction of the results of acts is dependent on it.[62]

The Vedānta-Sūtras IV 1,15 and 19 differentiate between *karma* which has not begun to bear fruits (*anārabdhakarma*) and *karma* which has begun to bear fruits (*ārabdhakarma*). The purpose of the latter is to explain why a person liberated while still alive remains alive for a very short time (*kaṃcit kālam*) although he is in possession of Brahma-vision. As soon as the *ārabdhakarma* is completely wiped out, deliverance through release from the body (*videhamukti*) takes place. If this is not the case, a new embodiment occurs (*evam eva prārabdhakarmābhāve śarīrapātānantaram eva mokṣas tadbhāve janmāntarāṇīty aniyamaḥ*).[63]

In principle, Madhva had two patterns at his disposal in order to explain the concepts of *ārabdhakarma* and *anārabdhakarma* in the context of liberation while alive, namely one put forward by Śaṅkara/Maṇḍana and the other, supported by Kumārila/Śrīdhara. While Śaṅkara and Maṇḍana were of the opinion that ultimate knowledge (*samyagjñāna/darśana*) wipes out only the *anārabdhakarma,* not the *ārabdhakarma* also, which is to be destroyed by fruition,[64] On the other hand, Kumārila and Śrīdhara criticized this Vedānta-view, which they refer to and refute as *pūrvapakṣa.* According to these latter

---

[61] Cf. Mesquita 2000: 506ff.

[62] It is interesting to note that Yogavāsiṣṭha makes no use at all of the concept of *karma* while explaining the concept of liberation while alive (cf. Slaje 2000: 177).

[63] BSūBh p. 191,7.

[64] Cf. Bos 1983: 167; BS p. 129,18.

authors, the ultimate knowledge destroys ignorance, and prevents the rise of new *karma.* The stockpile of karmic residues of previous lives as well as of the present life is destroyed gradually (*krameṇa*) by fruition and by performance of religious rites (*karmabhiś ca*).

Their statements expressing this criticism are based above all on the idea that the ultimate knowledge flares up all of a sudden and that there is no reason why the ultimate knowledge cannot destroy the entire stockpile of karmic residues regardless of their distinction (*aviśeṣāt*). In this case, the embodiment too, which is regarded as a product of *karma*, will cease to exist, and consequently the liberation while alive would be impossible.[65]

Madhva's opinion on the matter shows some distinctive features. In principle, he follows the *Vedānta*-teaching *ad* Sū IV 1,15: *anārabdhakārye eva pūrve puṇyapāpe vinaśyataḥ* / ...; but he supplements it with a quote from an unknown *Smṛti*-source. In his view, the teaching of this source is indicated already in the Sū by the particle *tu*:

> *tuśabdaḥ smṛtidyotakaḥ –*
> *yad anārabdhapāpaṃ syāt tad vinaśyati niścayāt* /
> *paśyato brahma nirdvandvaṃ hīnaṃ ca brahma paśyataḥ* /
> *dviṣato vā bhavet puṇyanāśo nāsty atra saṃśayaḥ* /
> *tasyāpy ārabdhakāryasya na vināśo 'sti kutracit* /
> *ārabdhayoś ca nāśaḥ syād alpayoḥ puṇyapāpayoḥ* /
> *iti ca nārāyaṇatantre.*

The particle 'but' points to the [following] *smṛti*:

---

[65] Cf. Mesquita 1994: 459 and 469f.; see also Mesquita 1995: 226f. It is interesting to note that this opinion is mentioned and refuted by Maṇḍana and Śaṅkara (cf. BS p. 130,6f. and BSūBh *ad* IV 1,15). See also a slightly different view of Vyomaśiva (cf. Mesquita 1995: 225n.38). Possibly, the criticism of Kumārila and Śrīdhara was also the reason why Jayatīrtha rejected altogether the concept of liberation while alive; cf. above n. 4.

> "In the case of a person, who has the vision of the independent Brahman, his evil deed, which did not begin to bear fruit, will surely be destroyed. And the destruction of [all] merit takes place in the case of one who looks down upon Brahman or hates Him. This is beyond doubt. In either case, there is also no destruction of *karma* which has begun to bear fruits. And the destruction of a negligible part of good or evil deeds, is possible [even] in the case of these [deeds], which have begun to bear fruits." This too has been said in the Nārāyaṇatantra.

The minimal deviations from the *Vedānta* doctrine, in the case of those [deeds], which have been mentioned above, namely that also an *ārabdhakarma* (good or evil), which is negligible, could be seized and destroyed by the ultimate knowledge,[66] cannot be interpreted as a compromise on the point criticized by Śrīdhara.[67] In any case, the above mentioned deviation will not, really speaking, remove the doubts expressed by Śrīdhara. It is strange that Madhva in the above quote speaks not only of a *jīvanmukta* but also of a soul doomed to hell.[68] He pursues this subject also in his commen-

---

[66] Somewhat amazing is the anonymous statement of Madhva (*ad* Sū IV 1) in NyāV (p. 207,13-14). It puts foward without curtailment the original *Vedānta*-teaching:

> *karmāṇi kṣapayed viṣṇur aprārabdhāni vidyayā* /
> *prārabdhāni tu bhogena kṣapayan svapadaṃ nayet* /
> *iti vacanāc ca.*

Almost in the same wording another statement of Madhva in SŚS (v. 22):

> *prārabdhakarmaṇo 'nyasya jñānena syāt parikṣayaḥ* /
> *aniṣṭasyobhayasyāpi sarvasyānyasya bhogataḥ* /.

[67] In BhāgTN p. 51,1-3 Madhva ascribes the above mentioned destruction to a great cause (= Bhakti): *jñāninām prārabdhasyaiva nirmathanam* / *yogasyaiva* –

> *mahatā kāraṇenaiva prārabdhāny api kānicit* /
> *karmāṇi kṣayam āyānti brahmadṛṣṭimataḥ kvacit* /
> *iti bhaviṣyatparvaṇi* (fictitious source).

[68] See also Anuv pp. 198,28-200,7: ... *iti sattattvavacanaṃ svayaṃ bhagavatoditam* (unknown source); Mesquita 2000: 527f.

tary on BSū (*ad* IV 1,19) invoking again the same unknown source as above:

> *ārabdhapuṇyapāpe bhogena kṣapayitvā brahma saṃpatsyate / atheti niyamasūcakaḥ –*
> *ārabdhapuṇyapāpasya bhogena kṣapaṇād anu /*
> *prāpnoty eva tamo ghoraṃ brahma vā nātra saṃśayaḥ /*
> *brahmaṇāṃ śatakālāt tu pūrvam ārabdhasaṃkṣayaḥ /*
> *niyamena bhaven nātra kāryā kācid vicāraṇā /*
> *iti ca nārāyaṇatantre.*

> Through the destruction of the good and evil *karma* which has begun to bear fruits, one attains Brahman. [The *pratīka*] *atha* (= then) points to a general rule [that one surely attains Brahman after destroying the *karma*]. And this is said in the Nārāyaṇatantra: "After destroying the good and evil *karma* which has begun to bear fruits through fruition, one attains Brahman or hell of darkness. This is beyond doubt. [The complete] destruction of *karma* which has begun to bear fruits could necessarily take place at [the end] of a hundred Brahmā-years. This is absolutely beyond question."

It is noteworthy that we find in this quote a facet of the doctrine of release which has been emphasized by Śrīdhara and Kumārila, namely that the period of time needed for the complete destruction of the karmic residues piled up along several births (*anekajanmasahasrasaṃcitāṇāṃ karmaṇām*) has no fixed time-limit (*kālāniyama*).[69] Regarding this point, a *śloka* from Kumārila's lost work Bṛhaṭṭīkā has been handed down:

> *kurvann ātmasvarūpajño bhogāt karmaparikṣayam /*
> *yugakoṭisahasreṇa kaścid eko vimucyate //*

> "A person in possession of the [true] knowledge of the nature of the Ātman, is released [only] after millions of

[69] This teaching is recorded also in the Purāṇas; cf. BrahVP II 26,69f.

aeons (*yuga*) since [all his] *karma* is destroyed through fruition."[70]

Madhva has fully absorbed this idea into his doctrine of liberation while alive. Like Kumārila, Madhva too rejects the doctrine of *mahāpralaya* which implies the annihilation of the entire karmic residues.[71] Accordingly, Madhva distinguishes between souls who attained the liberation while still alive in their last bodily state (*caramadeha*) and souls who are doomed to go through a long and tiresome path of liberation for innumerable births.[72] The souls predestined to liberation while alive have an unshakaable certitude (*mokṣaniyama*)[73] of their release, since they are *muktiyogya* due to their intrinsic aptitude (*yogyatājātikṛta*) conferred upon them by Viṣṇu.[74]
The first group of souls has completely deleted the karmic residues by fruition and by ultimate knowledge i.e. by vision of Viṣṇu, while the second group has to wait for the final liberation, which takes a long time until all the karmic residues are completely deleted and the souls finally attain the ultimate

---

[70] Cf. Mesquita 1994: 467f.; see also Gī VI 45 and below n. 75.

[71] Cf. Mesquita 2000: 469.

[72] Madhva describes this tiresomeness with the help of an unknown quotation in GīBh p. 46,22-24:

tathā hy uktam –
saṃskāro balavān eva brahmādyā api tadvaśāḥ /
tathāpi so'nyathākartuṃ śakyate'tiprayatnataḥ / iti

Anuv p. 163,10-12:

doṣā anādisaṃbadhās te muktiparipanthinaḥ /
santy eva prāyaśaḥ puṃsu tena mokṣo na jāyate /
sarve ta ete jīveṣu dṛśyante tāratamyataḥ /;

see also NK p. 676,7: *anādivāsanāvāsita itiprabalo nisargabaddhaḥ sarvaḥ sāṃvyavahārikaḥ pratyakṣeṇa pratyayaḥ* (Mesquita 1995: 222).

[73] Cf. above nn. 28; 42 and below p. 19 (*ad* Gī VI 31); BhāgTN p. 278,1-3:

ye jñānaviṣayāḥ śāpā muktigāś cādhikāriṇām /
kādācitkās te bhavanti naiva te sārvakālikāḥ /
teṣāṃ jñānasya mukteś ca tāratamyasya caiva ha /
bhagavanniyatatvāt tu śāpādir nātra kāraṇam /
iti vārahe (untraceable).

[74] According to the teachings of Madhva the classification of the souls in *muktiyogya*, *nityababdha* and *tamoyogya* goes back to the inscrutable decision of the Lord Viṣṇu; cf. Mesquita 2000: 510ff.

knowledge. This distinction is based on several explicit statements of Madhva himself. For instance, in his commentary on Gī (*ad* II 72) he speaks of a *jñānin*, who achieves liberation (*ato jñāninām bhavaty eva muktiḥ*) and also of another *jñānin* who will be reborn and will be finally released only after many rebirths: *jñāninām api sati prārabdhakarmaṇi śarīrāntaraṃ yuktam / bhogena tv itara iti hy uktam* (BSū IV 1,19) */ santi hi bahuśarīraphalāni karmāṇi kānicit / saptajanmani vipraḥ syād ityadeḥ* (Ṛgveda IX 67,190?) */ dṛṣṭeś ca jñāninām api bahuśarīraprāpteḥ*. We find a similar idea in different variations. For instance, in connection with Gī VI 45:[75]

jijñāsur jñātvā prayatnaṃ karoti / evam anekajanmabhiḥ saṃsiddho 'parokṣajñānī bhūtvā parāṃ gatim yāti / āha ca –
atīva śraddhayā yukto jijñāsur viṣṇutatparaḥ /
jñātvā dhyātvā tathā dṛṣṭvā janmabhir bahubhiḥ pumān /
viśen nārāyaṇaṃ devaṃ nānyathā tu kathaṃcana /
iti nāradīye (untraceable).
bahujanmavipākena bhaktijñānena ye harim /
bhajanti tatsmṛtiṃ tv ante devo yāti na cānyathā /
ity ukter brahmavaivarte (untraceable).[76]

---

[75] Gī VI 45:
prayatnād yatamānas tu yogī saṃśuddhakilbiṣaḥ /
anekajanmasaṃsiddhis tato yāti parāṃ gatim //
It is noteworty, that Śaṅkara too adopts this view in his Brahmasūtrabhāṣya (*ad* III 4,51) referring to the above mentioned śloka: *śravaṇādidvāreṇāpi vidyotpadyamānā pratibandhakṣayāpekṣayaivotpadyate / tathā ca śrutir durbodhatvam ātmano darśayati* (= KaU II 7) *garbhastha eva ca vāmadevaḥ pratipede brahmabhāvam iti* (= BĀU I 4,10) *vadantī janmāntarasaṃcitāt sādhanāj janmāntare vidyotpattiṃ darśayati / na hi garbhasthasyaivaihikaṃ kiṃcit sādhanaṃ saṃbhavyate / smṛtāv api* (= Gī VI 37cd/ 40cd/43ab and VI 45cd) *ity antenaitad darśayati / tasmād aihikam āmuṣmikaṃ vā vidyājanma pratibandhakṣayāpekṣayati sthitam.*

[76] GīBh p. 72,3-6; 36,8- 9 and 72,14-16:
ajñātvā dhyāyino dhyānāj jñānam eva viśiṣyate /
jñātvā dhyānaṃ jñānamātrād dhyānād api tu darśanam /
darśanāc caiva bhakteś ca na kiṃcit sādhanādhikam /
iti nāradīye (untraceable);
see also ibid. p. 39,6-12:

Such a conception implies that the distinguishing mark of a *jīvanmukta* consists of firm wisdom which is deeply grounded on Brahman and which is therefore an immediate knowledge (*aparokṣajñāna*) or a Brahma-vision.[77] On the other hand, the knowledge of a soul which is not released is not firm, since the influence of the *karma* that is still operating is mighty (*balavān*).[78]

For this reason, it will be reborn (*brāhmī sthitiḥ* {= Gī II 72} *brahmaviṣayā sthitir lakṣaṇam / antakāle 'pi asyāṃ sthitvaiva brahma gacchati / anyathā janmāntaraṃ prāpnoti*).[79] Thus, the characteristic mark (*liṅga*) of a soul which is not

---

...

jīvaṃś caturdaśād ūrdhvaṃ puruṣo niyamena tu /
strī vāpy anūnadaśakaṃ dehaṃ mānuṣam ārjate /
caturdaśordhvajīvini saṃsāraś cādivarjitaḥ /
ato 'vittvā paraṃ devaṃ mokṣāśā kā mahāmune /
iti brāhme (untraceable);

also BSūBh p. 191,9-11:

vidvān amṛtam āpnoti nātra kāryā vicaraṇā /
avasannaṃ yadārabdhaṃ karma tatraiva gacchati /
na ced bahūni janmāni prāpyaivānte na saṃśayaḥ /
iti ca nārāyaṇādhyātme.

77 Cf. GīBh p. 66,17f.; see also above p. 3.

78 Cf. GīBh p. 46,23f.; BhāgTN p. 51,10-11:

jñānādivyaktir avyaktiḥ sukhaduḥkhādikaṃ tathā /
sudṛṣṭabrahmatattvānāṃ bhavaty ārabdhakarmaṇā /
iti brahmavaivarte (untraceable).

It is suggested here, that even a knower of Brahman is not in possession of complete knowledge since he is still under the influence of *karma*. In the following, also untraceable quote, Madhva concedes that a knower of Brahman, as far as he has no affection for Viṣṇu, sometimes throws suspicion on the reality of the world:

bhagavantaṃ vinānyatra pravṛttyādiprakāśanam /
prārabdhakarmaṇaiva syāt kadācij jñāninām api /
tāṃ dvaitadṛṣṭiṃ me deva cchindhi jñānavarāsinā /
iti brāhme

Madhva speaks here of Advaitins! Elsewhere, he insinuates that the followers of opposing schools as Nyāya, etc. can attain the liberating knowledge only after many births (cf. GīBh p. 35,9-18; GīT p. 53,24-27 and Mesquita 2000. 521n. 688). The doctrine of two kind of *jñānins* has been expounded also by later Advaitins like Vidyāraṇya, namely as *jñānimātra* and as a *jñānin* with a firm wisdom (*sthitaprajña*); cf. Sprockhoff 1970: 137.

79 GīBh p. 35,8-9.

liberated consists in the fact that its immediate knowledge will arise at a later time or in a future birth. This is the reason why Madhva describes these persons by *aparokṣajñānarahitajñāninaḥ.*[80] This means that these persons will not attain liberation until their bhakti has ripened through several births (*bahujanmavipākena bhaktijñānena*).[81]

Consequently, this doctrine agrees with the principle held by Madhva that the way (*liṅgabhedana*) in which the release is achieved corresponds to the way in which *bhakti* operates. While in the case of a *jīvanmukta*, *bhakti* instantly brings about release, in the case of souls in bondage *bhakti* operates slowly, i.e. after many births:

yathā bhaktiviśeṣo 'tra dṛśyate puruṣottame /
tathā muktiviśeṣo 'pi jñāninām liṅgabhedane /[82]

The second characteristic mark of a *jīvanmukta* is that by definition, he is not able to perform evil deeds, inasmuch as he is absolutely free from all wordly desires (*vairāgya*) – *viraktānām eva ca jñānam* – and worldly desire is the seed of transmigrations (*saṃsārabīja*): *abandhakatvaṃ tv akāmenaiva bhavati.*[83] On the other hand, those souls which have not yet attained liberation while alive are not free from the seed of the

---

[80] Cf. GīBh p. 32,27f.; see also above n. 19.

[81] Cf. GīBh p. 72,3f. and above n. 75. Madhva seems to follow here closely the opinion of Kumārila and Śrīdhara that the current existence in which the release takes place is the result of the good deeds in the past lives or that the gradual increase of the intensive contemplation (*samādhi*) through concentration of thoughts produces a *dharma* which brings about a contemplation which is even more intense (*prakṛṣṭa*). The *dharma* which emerges from this contemplation is also active in the future lives (*janmāntare 'py anuvartate*); cf. Mesquita 1995: 238. In this sense Śaṅkara too, cf. above n. 75.

[82] Cf. GīT p. 30,14-16. In BSūBh p. 138,7-9 this quote has been simply identified without giving further details as *smṛti*; cf. above nn. 57-60.; see also BhāgTN p. 602,7-8:

kecid unmādavad bhaktā bāhyaliṅgapradarśakāḥ /
kecid āntarabhaktāḥ syuḥ kecic caivobhayātmakāḥ /
mukhaprasādāt dārḍhyāc ca bhaktir jneyā na cānyataḥ /
iti vārāhe (untraceable).

[83] Cf. above nn. 17; 28 and 34; see also Mesquita 1995: 246f.

transmigration, since their mind is normally not directed towards sense-objects: *na tasya manaḥ prāyo viṣayeṣu gacchati.*[84] For this reason, they sometimes succumb to *adharma.* Madhva refers to it in his GīBh (*ad* VI 31):

> *evam aparokṣaṃ paśyato jñānaphalaṃ niyatam ity arthaḥ / tathāpi prāyo nādharmaṃ karoti / kurvatas tu mahac ced duḥkhasūcakam bhavatīty uktaṃ purastāt / āha ca –*
> *kadācid api nādharme buddhir viṣṇudṛśāṃ bhavet /*
> *pramādāt tu kṛtaṃ pāpaṃ svalpaṃ bhasmībhaviṣyati /*
> *ādirājais tathā devair ṛṣibhiḥ kriyate kiyat /*
> *bāhulyāt karmaṇas teṣāṃ duḥkhasūcakam eva tat /*
> *iti* (unknown quote).

> When one has thus seen [Viṣṇu] directly, [this vision] always brings about the fruit of wisdom. This is the meaning. Yet a [*jñānin*] normally does not commit evil deeds. If, nevertheless, he commits a great [evil deed] pain is pointed out [for him as punishment]. This has been said earlier. And [for the sake of further clarification] it is also said: "The mind of those who possess the direct vision of Viṣṇu is never directed towards evil deeds. If however, through carelessness he [as *jñānin*] has commited some small evil acts, they get burnt out [through the vision of Viṣṇu]. Thus, any [minor evil deed] that is performed by ancient kings, gods [and] ṛṣis [will be burnt out through the vision of Viṣṇu]. Because of abundance [of such evil deeds] pain is indeed indicated [as punishment] for them."

It is obvious that this anonymous quote marks clear limits between two kind of *jñānin*-s: on the one hand, *jñānin*-s who either cannot commit grievous evil deeds (*kadācid api na* ...) or perhaps may commit minor evil deeds out of carelessness; and on the other hand, *jñānin*-s who commit grievous evil

[84] GīBh p. 66,16-17 and above n. 46.

deeds. The deeds of the former will be burnt out as a result of the vision of Viṣṇu[85] and hence they will not have to suffer any pain. The latter, by contrast, will have to endure pains, and therefore they will be reborn. The sins of these have a longer existence in the form of *ārabdhakarma*, which comprises not only *pāpa* but also *puṇya* or *jñāna/bhakti,* which remain active during countless lives, building a basis for a future *jīvanmukti.* In another anonymuous quote Madhva draws attention to the distinction between the two different types of *jñānins.* Possibly, Madhva pointed to it earlier as indicated by the remark: *ity uktaṃ purastāt* (Gī *ad* VI 4):

> *uktaṃ ca –*
> *svato doṣalayo dṛṣṭyā tv itareṣāṃ prayatnataḥ / iti*

In other words, the minor sins incurred through carelessness will be burnt out by the Viṣṇu-vision, while the deletion of greater sins occurs only through a continued exertion (*prayatnataḥ*) by way of several births and rebirths.[86]

In this sense, it is also said in BSūBh (*ad* IV 1.13): *brahmadarśana uttarāghasyāśleṣaḥ pūrvasya vināśaś ca* (= ChU IV 14,3 and V 24,3) *iti tadvyapadeśāt.* Madhva relates it with another untraceable quote ascribed to a Purāṇa:

> *yathāśleṣo vināśaś ca muktasya tu vikarmaṇaḥ /*
> *evaṃ sukarmaṇaś cāpi patatas tamasi dhruvaḥ /*
> *iti cāgneye.*

---

[85] See also Anuv p. 198,28-29:

> *tasmād yathoktamārgeṇa brahmopāsyaṃ mumukṣibhiḥ /*
> *tathopāsyāñjasā dṛṣṭaṃ brahma pāpaṃ ca bhasmasāt /*
> *karoti nikhilaṃ pūrvaṃ paścāt yasyāpy asaṅgatām /*
> *karoti ...*

[86] See also BSūBh p. 199,7-9:

> *anabhīṣṭam anārabdhaṃ puṇyam apy asya naśyati /*
> *kiṃ tu pāpaṃ parabrahmajñānino nāsti saṃsayaḥ /*
> *iti pādme* (untraceable).

See also above n. 75 and BhāgTN p. 266,8-9:

> *tattvajñānaṃ tu devānāṃ garbhasthānāṃ bhaviṣyati /*
> *uttamānām ṛṣīṇaṃ vāpy anyeṣāṃ bahujanmagam /*
> *iti skānde* (untraceable).

In connection with the points discussed above, Madhva gives a well-defined image of a *jīvanmukta*, namely, a person without even a spot of sin, without loss (*hāni*) of direct knowledge who, nevertheless, has to bear the painful consequences of his previous sins, as long as he remains in bondage:

> *vikarmalepo naivāsti samyagdṛṣṭimatāṃ kvacit /*
> *guṇahāniś ca naivāsti brahmaṇas tv avikarmataḥ /*
> ...
> *apāpatvaṃ ca naivāsti yāvat saṃsāram asya hi /*
> *ārabdhapāpam asty eva duḥkhaṃ ca jñānino 'pi hi /.*[87]

Having come to the end of our investigation of all the aspects of the doctrine of liberation while alive according to Madhva, we can note, first of all, that our author not only uses the technical term for liberation while still alive but also explains it at length quoting from innumerable sources. The special feature of these sources is that they are either completely unknown or, if they are known, the quotes are all with no exception, untraceable. By liberation while alive Madhva understands an irreversible state of highest happiness (*ānandarūpa*) or a final perfection which is achieved through direct knowledge of Brahman/Viṣṇu (*aparokṣajñāna/brahmadarśana*). *Aparokṣajñāna* destroys completely ignorance and *anārabdhakarma*. Moreover, it prevents the rise of new *karma*. The remnants of *prārabdhakarma*, which keep the *jīvanmukta* alive, are destroyed by fruition and by the performance of devotional works until the hour of death.[88] Since the entire karmic residues are deleted in this supreme hour, *videhamukti* follows

---

[87] Anuv pp. 173,15 and 174,18-19; MBhTN I 127-129:
> *yadā muktipradānasya svayogaṃ paśyati dhruvam /*
> *rūpaṃ hares tadā tasya sarvapāpāni bhasmasāt /*
> *yānti pūrvāṇy uttarāni na śleṣaṃ yānti kānicit /*
> *mokṣaś ca niyatas tasmāt svayogyaharidarśane /*
> *bhaviṣyaparvavacanam ity etat sūtragaṃ* (IV 1,13) *tathā* [fictitious source].

[88] Cf. above nn. 22, 27, 39, 47 and 49.

immediately.[89] It is worth noting in this connection that Madhva lays stress on the fact that not only *videhamukti* but also *jīvanmukti* are not the fruits of human effort or merely a result of the fruition of *prārabdhakarma* but an act of mercy, a gift of God Viṣṇu. In this sense, Madhva acknowledges that liberation is absolutely dependent on Viṣṇu's free will when he declares: *nāham kartā hariḥ kartā ... tathāpi matkṛtā pujā tatprasādena nānyathā ...* Another statement of his runs: *narte tvat kriyate kiṃcid ityāder na hariṃ vinā ... ajñānāṃ jñānado viṣṇur jñānīnāṃ mokṣadaś ca ... ānandaś ca muktāṇāṃ sa evaiko janārdanaḥ.*[90]

Aparokṣajñāna, as synonymous with *jīvanmukti*, which Madhva sometimes substitutes by *brahmadarśana* and *samādhyādiphala*,[91] could be interpreted as a mystical vision, where the identity of the individual soul remains unaffected. Thus, Madhva refrains from taking up the opinion of Śaṅkara. In contrast to the Advaitins, Madhva advocated that a *jīvanmukta* has not even a slight trace of ignorance (*ajñānaleśa*). Advaitins

---

[89] In support of this doctrine Madhva again cites unknown or untraceable quotes, cf. AiUBh p. 220,19-22:

anārabdhaphalānāṃ ca prārabdhānāṃ ca sarvaśaḥ /
karmaṇāṃ dāha evāyaṃ muktir ity abhidhīyate /
sa tu muktas tato dehād udgacchati parātmanā /
prerito viṣṇulokaṃ ca prāpya bhogān avāpya ca /
bhuṅkte viṣṇuprasādena na viṣṇor avaśaḥ kvacit /
viṣṇutantrā ime sarve muktā api yato 'khilāḥ /
iti brahmāṇḍe (untraceable);

BSūBh p. 191,7-11 (= cf. above n. 76); BhāgTN p. 52,3-5:

prakṛtiṃ svātmasaṃśliṣṭāṃ guṇān sattvādikān api /
karmāṇi sūkṣmadehaṃ ca jāyamānā harer dṛśiḥ /
dahed athāpi vai dagdhendhanavad tat punaḥ punaḥ /
yāvad ārabdhakarma syād āvir vāpi tiro vrajed /
iti brahmatarke (fictitious source).

See also SŚS (v. 23f.) and Mesquita 2000: 520n. 688.

[90] Cf. nn. 52-53. In view of this clear assertion of Madhva, it is difficult to grasp why Jayatīrtha rejected the concept of *jīvanmukti* on the ground that the destruction of the *prārabdakarma* through fruition and through performance of devotional works (cf. n. 88) would obstruct the free will of Viṣṇu (cf. above n. 4.).

[91] Cf. v. g. above p. 5f.

like Vimuktātman had postulated it in a *jīvanmukta*: *ato 'jñānaleśād eva tadvidaḥ śarīrādyābhāsa eṣṭavyaḥ*.[92]

We have solid reasons to assume that Madhva developed his teachings of *jīvanmukti* under the influence of non-advaita authors,[93] such as Kumārila and Śrīdhara. The fact that he sometimes takes up slightly divergent views is closely connected with the unknown or fictitious literary sources from which he quotes in order to justify these views.[94] It is therefore not surprising that Madhva relies exclusively on unknown and fictitious sources,[95] in order to support his particular views. In the case of the doctrine of *jīvanmukti* too Madhva does not show his power of thinking creatively, but demonstrates a high degree of imagination in making use of traditional thought-patterns. The fact that he has chosen terms like *pūrṇaprajña* (= *sthitaprajña/aparokṣajñānin*), *sarvajñamuni* and *sarvajñasūrya*[96]

---

[92] Cf. IS p. 76,9-13; see also Mesquita 2000: 181n. 375. Prakāśātman was of the opinion that it was also Śaṅkara's and Padmapāda's view (cf. Cammann 1965: 163; Bos 1983: 172f.). This applies also to Maṇḍana (cf. Oberhammer 1994: 58-61).

[93] Sheridan (1996: 91f. and 94f.), on the contrary, opines that Madhva sketched his doctrine of *jīvanmukti* under the influence of Śaṅkara.

[94] Cf. above n. 13.

[95] Cf. Mesquita 2000_1: 20f.; 45n. 61 [= 1997: 17f.; 37n. 53]. It is striking that Madhva's unknown or fictitious quotes regarding the liberation while alive very often end with phrases like *nānyathā tu kathaṃcana*. These expressions which Madhva uses also in connection with his other teachings (cf. Mesquita 2000_1: 169f. [= 1997: 137f]. underline the uniqueness of his doctrine. In the case of liberation while alive too my observation finds confirmation in the fact that the unknown or fictitious quotes of Madhva have been composed by himself as befitting the occasion and have been assigned sometimes to well known sources and sometimes to fictitious sources. From time to time he has re-worked the literary passages handed down in the tradition to fit in with his own doctrine (Mesquita 2000_1: 172 [=1997: 139]).

[96] Cf. BhāgTN p. 584,13-14:

> *samyagjñānavadācāryān mucyate puruṣo bhavāt /*
> *dvāv eva nityamuktau tu paramaḥ prakṛtis tathā /*
> *iti vāmane* (untraceable).

See also above n. 18; Mesquita 2000_1: 177n. 374 [= 1997: 143n. 360]. Madhva's direct disciples, such as Trivikramapaṇḍitācārya, paid tribute to his authority as an omniscient teacher in his subcommentary to Madhva's BSūBh, Tattvapradīpikā (ed. K. T. Pandurangi, Bangalore 1997, vol. I, p.

shows that Madhva firmly believed himself to be a *jīvan-muktaḥ*.

4,16-19; 52f.): ... *ācāryaḥ svoktārthe svayam eva pramāṇam sarvajñatvād avipralambhakatvāc ca ... sarvajñatvaṃ tāvat śrutisiddham* (= ṚV I 141,1-5; see also Mesquita 2000_1: 54f. [=1997: 43f.].

BIBLIOGRAPHY AND ABBREVIATIONS

1) Primary Sources

Anuv	*Anuvyākhyāna* des Madhva, in *Sarvamūlagranthāḥ – Prasthānatrayī*, Vol. 1, ed. B. Govindacharya, Udipi 1969. (Works of Sri Madhwacharya)
IS	Vimuktātman, *Iṣṭasiddhi with Extracts from the Vivaraṇa of Jñānottama*. Ed. M. Hiriyanna. Baroda 1933.
AiUBh	*Aitareyopaniṣadbhāṣya* des Madhva, s. *Anuv*.
KaU	*Kaṭhopaniṣad*, s. *BĀU*.
KūrmaP	*Kūrmapurāṇa*. Ed. Nag Sharan Singh. Delhi 1983.
Gī	*Bhagavadgītā*, s. *MBh*.
GīT	*Bhagavadgītātātparya* des Madhva, s. *Anuv*.
GīBh	*Bhagavadgītābhāṣya* des Madhva, s. *Anuv*.
GīBhŚ	*Gītābhāṣya* des Śaṅkara. Ed. D.V. Gokhale. Poona 1950.
CS	*Citsukhī* [=] *Tattvapradīpikā* des Citsukha mit *Nayaprasādinī* des Pratyaksvarūpa. Ed. Svamin Yogindrananda. Kashi 1956.
ChU	*Chāndogyopaniṣad*, s. *BĀU*.
ChUBh	*Chāndogyopaniṣadbhāṣya* des Madhva, s. *Anuv*.
NK	*Nyāyakandalī* des Śrīdhara, in *Praśastapādabhāṣya with the Commentary Nyāyakandalī by Śrīdharabhaṭṭa along with Hindi Translation by D. Jha*. Varanasi 1963.
NyāBh	*Nyāyabhūṣaṇa* des Bhāsarvajña. Ed. Svamin Yogindrananda. Varanasi 1968. (Ṣaḍdarśanagranthamālā 1)
NyāV	*Nyāyavivaraṇa* des Madhva, s. *Anuv*.
BĀU	*Bṛhadāraṇyakopaniṣad*, in *Eighteen Principal Upaniṣads*, Vol. 1, ed. V.P. Limaye and R.D. Vadekar, Poona 1958.
BrahVP	*Brahmavaivartapurāṇa* Parts 1-2. Ed. J.L. Shastri. Delhi 1983-1985.
BS	*Maṇḍanamiśra, Brahmasiddhi with Commentary by Śaṅkhapāṇi*. Ed. K. Sastri. Madras 1937.
BSū	*Brahmasūtra*, s. *BSūBh*.
BSūBh	*Brahmasūtrabhāṣya* des Madhva, s. *Anuv*.

BSūBhŚ — *Brahmasūtrabhāṣya* des Śaṅkara. Ed. J.L. Shastri. Delhi 1980.

BhāgTN — *Bhāgavatatātparyanirṇaya* des Madhva, in *Sarvamūlagranthāḥ – Purāṇaprasthāna*, Vol. 3, ed. B. Govindacharya, Udipi 1980. (Works of Sri Madhwacharya)

BhāgP — *Bhāgavatapurāṇa with Sanskrit Commentary Bhāvārthabodhinī of Śrīdhara*. Ed. J.L. Shastri. Delhi 1983.

MatsyaP — *Matsyapurāṇa*. 2 vols. Ed. Nag Sharan Singh. Delhi 1983.

MuUBh — *Muṇḍakopaniṣadbhāṣya* des Madhva, s. *Anuv*.

MBh — *Mahābhārata. Text as Constituted in its Critical Edition*. 4 vols. Poona 1971-1975.

MBhTN — *Mahābhāratatātparyanirṇaya* des Madhva, in *Sarvamūlagranthāḥ – Itihāsaprasthāna*, Vol. 2, ed. B. Govindacharya, Udipi 1971.

MS — *Manusmṛti*. Ed. J.L. Shastri. Delhi 1990.

ŚBh — *Śrībhāṣya*. 2 vols. Ed. U.T. Viraraghavacharya. Madras 1967.

SŚS — *Sarvaśāstrārthasaṅgraha* des Madhva, s. *Anuv*.

2) Secondary Sources

Bos, M.
1983 — "After the Rise of Knowledge (Some Remarks Concerning Śaṅkara's Views on Jīvanmukti)." *Wiener Zeitschrift für die Kunde Südasiens* 27: 165-184.

Bronkhorst, J.
1998 — *Two Sources of Indian Asceticism*. Delhi.

Cammann, K.
1983 — *Das System des Advaita nach der Lehre Prakāśātmans*. Wiesbaden.

Dasgupta, S.
1975 — *A History of Indian Philosophy*. 5 vols. Delhi (first Indian edition).

Fort, A.O.
1998. *Jīvanmukti Transformation: Embodied Liberation in Advaita and Neo-Vedanta.* New York.

Fort, A.O. und P.Y. Mumme (eds.)
1996 *Living Liberation in Hindu Thought.* New York.

Garbe, R.
1894 *Die Sāmkhya-Philosophie.* Leipzig.

Hiriyanna, M.
1951 *Essentials of Indian Philosophy.* London.

Mesquita, R.
1994 "Die Idee der Erlösung bei Kumārilabhaṭṭa." In: Roque Mesquita und Chlodwig H. Werba (eds.), *Orbis Indicus: Festschrift für Gerhard Oberhammer* (= *Wiener Zeitschrift für die Kunde Südasiens* 38), Wien, pp. 451-484.
1995 "Der *Apavarga*-Begriff bei Śrīdhara. Eine vedāntische Erlösungslehre?" In: Mirja Jantunen, William L. Smith and Carl Suneson (eds.), *Sauhṛdyamaṅgalam: Studies in Honour of Siegfried Lienhard on his 70th Birthday*, Stockholm, pp. 215-258.
1997 *Madhva und seine unbekannten literarischen Quellen: Einige Beobachtungen.* Wien.
2000 *Madhva: Viṣṇutattvanirṇaya. Annotierte Übersetzung mit Studie.* Wien.
2000_1 *Madhva's Unknown Literary Sources: Some Observations.* New Delhi.

Oberhammer, G.
1971 *Yāmunamunis Interpretation von Brahmasūtram 2,2, 42-45: Eine Untersuchung zur Pañcarātra-Tradition der Rāmānuja-Schule.* Wien.
1984 *Wahrheit und Transzendenz.* Wien.
1994 *La Délivrance, dès cette vie (jīvanmukti).* Paris.

Puthiadam, I.
1985 *Viṣṇu the Ever Free: A Study of the Mādhava Concept of God.* Madras.

Radhakrishnan, S.
1929 *Indian Philosophy.* 2 vols. London.

Sheridan, D.P.
1996 "Direct Knowledge of God and Living Liberation in the Religious Thought of Madhva." In: A.O. Fort und P.Y. Mumme 1996: 91-112.

Siauve, S.
1957 *La voie vers la connaissance de Dieu (Brahma-Jijñāsā) selon l'anuvyākhyāna de Madhva.* Pondichéry.
1968 *La doctrine de Madhva: Dvaita-Vedānta.* Pondichéry.

Sinha, J.
1952 *A History of Indian Philosophy.* 2 vols. Calcutta.

Slaje, W.
1986 "*niḥśreyasam* im alten Nyāya." *Wiener Zeitschrift für die Kunde Südasiens* 30: 163-177.
1994 *Vom Mokṣopāyaśāstra zum Yogavāsiṣṭha-Mahārāmāyaṇa: Philologische Untersuchungen zur Entwicklungs- und Überlieferungsgeschichte eines indischen Lehrwerks mit Anspruch auf Heilsrelevanz.* Wien.
2000 "Liberation from Intentionality and Involvement: On the Concept of *jīvanmukti* according to the Mokṣopāya." *Journal of Indian Philosophy* 28: 171-194.

Sprockhoff, J.F.
1970 "Der Weg zur Erlösung bei Lebzeiten, ihr Wesen und ihr Wert nach dem Jīvanmuktiviveka des Vidyāraṇya." *Wiener Zeitschrift für die Kunde Südasiens* 14: 131-157.
1962 "Zur Idee der Erlösung bei Lebzeiten." *Numen* 9: 201-227.

Vetter, T.
1995 "Bei Lebzeiten das Todlose erreichen: Zum Begriff *amata* im alten Buddhismus." In: G. Oberhammer (ed.), *Im Tod gewinnt der Mensch sein Selbst: Das Phänomen des Todes in asiatischer und abendländischer Religionstradition. Arbeitsdokumentation eines Symposiums*, Wien, pp. 211-230.